THE
40-DAY

SURRENDER
FAST

Journal

Releasing What Separates You from
God's Plan for Your Best Life

CELESTE OWENS, PH.D.

Good Success Publishing

The 40-Day Surrender Fast Journal
Copyright © 2014 by Celeste Owens
Revised copyright © 2018 by Celeste Owens

This book is also available as an ebook. Visit www.surrenderfast.com.

Requests for information should be addressed to:
Good Success Publishing, P.O. Box 5072, Upper Marlboro, MD 20775

ISBN: 978-0-9978332-6-3 (hardcover)

Library of Congress Control Number: 2011933636

This book is printed on acid-free paper.

Cover design: August Pride, LLC
Interior design: Alexey Zgola

Printed in the United States of America

My Promise

*In the next **40** days, and with God's help,
I commit my time and my energy to surrendering
my entire being to Him.*

Your Name

Partner's Name

Date

CONTENTS

INTRODUCTION

elcome to the Surrender Fast!

This journal is the companion guide to *The 40-Day Surrender Fast* and is designed to capture all that God will do in and through you for the next 40 days.

You are embarking on the journey of a lifetime and for some of you this is literary the quiet before the destiny storm; the time of preparation before you transition into the greatest season of your life.

Mark Batterson wrote in *Draw the Circle*, "The shortest pencil is longer than the longest memory." In other words, God is going to do so many amazing things for you during the course of this Fast, that trusting your memory to store it all would be a mistake. You are encouraged to take time to journal this experience for a remembrance of His goodness.

JOURNAL GUIDELINES

Here are a few tips to assist you in creating a journal habit:

1. **Define "journaling"**. Truthfully, there is no perfect way to journal. As long as you write something down that is all that counts. Remember to start each day with prayer, the reading of *The 40-Day Surrender Fast* devotional and your Bible and answer the questions in the journal. If you don't have answers for every question or specific prayer request for a particular day, skip those sections. No pressure; just you and God enjoying your time together.

2. **Journal at the same time each day**. To develop a journaling habit it's often important to be consistent. Therefore, it is suggested that you journal the same time each day. The time of day doesn't matter as much as the process of journaling. If you have to journal in the evening, that's fine. Just do it.

3. **Set your alarm.** Now that you have picked a time of day, set your alarm. Life happens and pretty soon your enthusiasm for this Fast will fade in the minutia of every day routine and pressure. Setting your alarm will help you remain consistent when life gets in the way.

4. **Enjoy the journey.** Don't be too hard on yourself during the 40 days. A closer walk with God, not perfection is the goal. Therefore, seek Him with all your heart, surrender your will for His, and watch Him do the miraculous in your life.

Let God Do a New Thing!

POINT TO PONDER: I won't leave this year the same way I came in. The former things have passed; God wants to do a new thing in me.

SCRIPTURES TO REFERENCE: Isaiah 43:18-19

QUESTIONS TO ANSWER:

1. What "new thing" does God want to do in and for you?

_____

_____

_____

_____

_____

_____

2. Like Dr. Celeste, do you sense that God is asking you to give up some tasks or jobs that are important to you? Will you comply?

_____

_____

_____

_____

_____

3. What role, if any, will fear play in hindering you from allowing God to do the new thing in your life?

_____

_____

_____

_____

_____

_____

Prayer request(s):

_____

_____

_____

_____

_____

_____

How my prayer(s) was answered:

_____

_____

_____

_____

_____

_____

What Is a Surrender Fast?

POINT TO PONDER: I will no longer be stuck, frustrated, or bound. I am going to let God do something new in me and the blessings that will stem from my obedience will be well worth the sacrifice.

SCRIPTURES TO REFERENCE: Deuteronomy 28; Matthew 4:1-11

QUESTIONS TO ANSWER:

1. Dr. Celeste was introduced to fasting as a child and has continued the practice into adulthood. However, some new or even seasoned converts for that matter don't regard fasting as beneficial. What are your thoughts about fasting? Have you fasted in the past and did it produce the results you expected? What do you expect from this fast?

_____

_____

_____

_____

_____

_____

2. What area(s) of your life do you need to surrender to God? What will be most challenging about surrendering?

_____

_____

_____

_____

_____

3. How might this surrender change your relationship with yourself, God, and others?

_____

_____

_____

_____

Prayer request(s):

_____

_____

_____

_____

How my prayer(s) was answered:

_____

_____

_____

_____

Bold and Courageous

POINT TO PONDER: I am healed from the pains and wounds of the past; I am new in Christ, and equipped to succeed in all that I put my hands to.

SCRIPTURES TO REFERENCE: Isaiah 54:3-6; Isaiah 61:7

QUESTIONS TO ANSWER:

1. Have you decided what you will surrender for the next 40 days? If yes, write it below. If no, don't worry. Just continue to seek God's direction and He will give you the answer.

   _____

   _____

   _____

   _____

2. Like Dr. Celeste who was encouraged by the words God spoke to Joshua, how has God prepared your heart for such a fast?

   _____

   _____

   _____

   _____

   _____

3. The enemy wants you to be ashamed of your weaknesses and to hide them from others, but that philosophy only delays your healing. Therefore, identify a weakness and make arrangements to talk with at least one other person about it. Ask him/her to hold you accountable (through the duration of the fast) as you allow God to change you in this area.

_____

_____

_____

_____

4. If you can't readily identify a person that can be part of this process with you, pray. God will reveal the right person to you. When He does go to that person, explain what you are doing, and ask them to be part of this journey with you. List the name of that person here.

_____

_____

_____

_____

Prayer request(s):

_____

_____

_____

How my prayer(s) was answered:

_____

_____

_____

Why 40 Days?

POINT TO PONDER: In and of myself I am hopeless to change, but with God all things are possible. His healing virtue is tearing down the walls that have kept me confined and His grace is propelling me further than I ever thought I could go.

SCRIPTURES TO REFERENCE: Genesis 7:4; 1 Samuel 17:16; 2 Samuel 5:4; 1 Kings 2:11; Joshua 5:6; Matthew 4:2; Mark 1:14; Mark 9:14-29; Luke 4:2

QUESTIONS TO ANSWER:

1. What behaviors or circumstances keep you bound and also act as a barrier to the life God has for you?

_____

_____

_____

_____

_____

2. Do you believe that God can deliver you from any and every stronghold? Think of a behavior or habit that that you would like to eliminate. What have you tried in the past to rid yourself of this

problem? Has the problem gotten better over time or remained the same? How will you know when God has healed you?

_____

_____

_____

_____

_____

3. Are you willing to commit to this period of fasting for 40 days? What people or circumstances might negatively impact your ability to succeed at this fast?

_____

_____

_____

_____

_____

Prayer request(s):

_____

_____

_____

_____

How my prayer(s) was answered:

_____

_____

_____

_____

It's Complicated

POINT TO PONDER: I don't need anyone to approve of or accept me because God loves me just the way I am. If I meditate on His word day and night, do all that it says, I will make my way prosperous and I will have good success.

SCRIPTURES TO REFERENCE: Joshua 1:8; 2 Corinthians 10:5; I John 4:19.

QUESTIONS TO ANSWER:

1. What lies, if any, from childhood have you accepted as truth? In what ways do they continue to influence your thoughts and behavior?

_____

_____

_____

_____

_____

2. Do these lies also affect your current relationships? If yes, with whom and in what way?

_____

_____

_____

_____

_____

_____

3. How would you like for God to change you over the next 40 days?

_____

_____

_____

_____

_____

_____

Prayer request(s):

_____

_____

_____

_____

_____

How my prayer(s) was answered:

_____

_____

_____

_____

_____

Expect the Unexpected

"For My thoughts are not your thoughts,
nor are your ways my ways," says the LORD.
"For as the heavens are higher than the earth,
So are My ways higher than your ways,
And My thoughts than your thoughts.
(Isaiah 55:8-9)

POINT TO PONDER: Growth won't occur by osmosis; a dream comes with much business and painful effort. If I want to experience a new thing in God, I must do my part.

SCRIPTURES TO REFERENCE: Psalm 25:9, 69:32, 147:6; Ecclesiastes 5:3; Isaiah 55:8-9; James 4:10; I Peter 5:6

QUESTIONS TO ANSWER:

1. From the start God is instructing us to be humble. What does humility mean to you? How is it related to the act of surrender?

_____

_____

_____

_____

_____

2. Sometimes people are afraid to display humility because they associate meekness with weakness. Is there a difference between humility and being a pushover? How would you explain the difference?

_____

_____

_____

_____

_____

3. On a scale from one to ten, what is your commitment level to reading God's word daily, reading this devotional and praying? Explain your ranking.

_____

_____

_____

_____

_____

_____

Prayer request(s):

_____

_____

_____

_____

How my prayer(s) was answered:

_____

_____

_____

_____

Time, Effort, Reward

Sow for yourselves righteousness;
Reap in mercy;
Break up your fallow ground,
For it is time to seek the LORD,
Till He comes and rains righteousness on you.
(Hosea 10:12)

POINT TO PONDER: The new thing I seek is here, but my possession of it requires time and effort. This little investment of my time will reap an abundant reward!

SCRIPTURES TO REFERENCE: Hosea 10:12; Galatians 6:7; 2 Corinthians 9:6

QUESTIONS TO ANSWER:

1. What sacrifices will you make in order to draw closer to God?

    _____

    _____

    _____

2. Typically what is your commitment level when it comes to starting new regiments? Are you readily committed to a plan

from the beginning and follow it through to the end? Or are you commitment phobic? If the latter, what do you fear about commitment?

_____

_____

_____

_____

3. If you have identified fears, discuss them with your accountability partner. Pray and ask God to strengthen you so that you are able to push through the fear and succeed to the finish. If you are naturally a committed person, thank God for this gift and ask Him how He would like to use you to help develop this character trait in others.

_____

_____

_____

_____

Prayer request(s):

_____

_____

_____

_____

How my prayer(s) was answered:

_____

_____

_____

_____

DAY 3

Rebuild and Renew

And they shall rebuild the old ruins,
they shall raise up the former desolations,
And they shall repair the ruined cities,
The desolations of many generations.
(Isaiah 61:4)

POINT TO PONDER: My radical act of faith is doing the impossible. My surrender delights God.

SCRIPTURES TO REFERENCE: Psalm 37:4; Isaiah 61; Ephesians 3:20

QUESTIONS TO ANSWER:

1. Dr. Celeste mentioned some of the benefits of surrendering: more intimate relationship with God, improved emotional health, and breakthroughs in many other areas of your life. Can you think of any other benefits?

    _____

    _____

    _____

    _____

    _____

2. What impossible thing has God done for you in the past? What was that and how did it increase your faith?

_____

_____

_____

_____

_____

3. What abundant thing will God do for you and your family as a result of this fast? What generational curses are you asking Him to break? Do you believe that He can and will do it?

_____

_____

_____

_____

_____

Prayer request(s):

_____

_____

_____

_____

How my prayer(s) was answered:

_____

_____

_____

_____

The Other Side

On the same day, when evening had come, He said to them,
"Let us cross over to the other side."
(Mark 4:35)

POINT TO PONDER: Whatever He has asked me to release to
Him is His will and I will succeed.

SCRIPTURES TO REFERENCE: Mark 4:35-41; I Corinthians
2:9

QUESTIONS TO ANSWER:

1. What storms have begun in your life as a result of your surrender?

  _____

  _____

  _____

  _____

  _____

2. What can the disciples teach you about enduring the storm?

  _____

  _____

  _____

  _____

_____

_____

_____

3. Like Dr. Celeste, is God requiring you to step out of your comfort zone; to do some activities that you are fearful of doing? How long have you avoided this activity? Will you finally heed His voice?

_____

_____

_____

_____

_____

Prayer request(s):

_____

_____

_____

_____

How my prayer(s) was answered:

_____

_____

_____

_____

It Will Come to Pass

Every word of God is pure;
He is a shield to those who put their trust in Him.
(Proverbs 30:5)

POINT TO PONDER: God's word will not return to Him void.

SCRIPTURES TO REFERENCE: Joshua 21:45, 23:14; Proverbs 30:5; Zechariah 4:10; Matthew 25:23; I John 3:2a

QUESTIONS TO ANSWER:

1. What promises have God spoken to you that have yet to come to pass? Do you believe that He will do just as He has said?

   _____

   _____

   _____

   _____

   _____

2. What preparations are you making for the manifestation of each promise?

   _____

   _____

   _____

_____

_____

_____

_____

3. Sometimes as we wait we become anxious for the manifestation of God's plan. Are you content with today or anxious for tomorrow? If the latter, what will you do to maintain balance as you wait?

_____

_____

_____

_____

_____

_____

Prayer request(s):

_____

_____

_____

_____

How my prayer(s) was answered:

_____

_____

_____

_____

DAY 6

Personal Time with God

Scripture(s):

_____

_____

_____

_____

_____

How is the spirit speaking to you?

_____

_____

_____

_____

_____

DAY 7

Personal Time with God

Scripture(s):

_____

_____

_____

_____

_____

How is the spirit speaking to you?

_____

_____

_____

_____

_____

Establish Your Faith

And whatever you ask in My name, that I will do,
that the Father may be glorified in the Son.
If you ask anything in My name, I will do it.
(John 14:13-14)

POINT TO PONDER: Faith is more than mere words; it is an attitude of confidence that knows without a shadow of a doubt that God will do just as He has promised.

SCRIPTURES TO REFERENCE: Proverbs 18:21; John 14:13-14; Hebrews 11:6; James 2:20, 3:10

QUESTIONS TO ANSWER:

1. Establishing or activating your faith is only possible when you believe that God will do just what He has said. How convinced are you that God will work things out for your good? In which areas of your life do you need to trust God more?

_____

_____

_____

_____

_____

2. The scripture tells us that faith without works is dead (see James 2:26) . What does that mean to you? In which areas of your life do you need to establish your faith?

_____

_____

_____

_____

_____

3. There is power in sharing with another trusted individual what you believe God will do for you. Tell your accountability partner what you are expecting God to do.

_____

_____

_____

_____

_____

Prayer request(s):

_____

_____

_____

_____

How my prayer(s) was answered:

_____

_____

_____

_____

DAY 9

Pray for Your Enemies

Do not rejoice when your enemy falls,
And do not let your heart be glad when he stumbles;
Lest the LORD see it, and it displease Him,
And He turn away His wrath from him.
(Proverbs 24:17-18)

POINT TO PONDER: It's easy to love those who love me, but the proof of my conversion is reflected in my ability to love those who use me, who take advantage of my kindness, and wish harm upon me.

SCRIPTURES TO REFERENCE: Proverbs 24:17-18; Matthew 5:44; Philippians 4:13

QUESTIONS TO ANSWER:

1. Pray and ask God to reveal to you the condition of your heart. A prayer that I often whisper is, "God show me, me." Is He revealing to you a person or persons that you have not forgiven? If yes, what will you do to make this right?

_____

_____

_____

_____

_____

2. Forgiveness for those who have hurt us goes against our nature.
    Why then does God require us to forgive? What are the benefits
    of forgiving? What are the consequences of unforgiveness? Find
    scriptures to validate your answers.

    _____

    _____

    _____

    _____

    _____

3. What does Christ's sacrifice mean to you and how does it
    demonstrate how you are to love?

    _____

    _____

    _____

    _____

    _____

Prayer request(s):

_____

_____

_____

How my prayer(s) was answered:

_____

_____

_____

DAY 10

Renewal is Necessary

And He said to them,
"Come aside by yourselves to a deserted place and rest a while."
For there were many coming and going,
and they did not even have time to eat.
(Mark 6:31)

POINT TO PONDER: God wants me to live in the peace that surpasses all understanding, to have unspeakable joy, and to prosper in all things.

SCRIPTURES TO REFERENCE: Mark 6:30-32

QUESTIONS TO ANSWER:

1. Based on Dr. Celeste's definition, are you primarily busy or primarily productive? If you are prone to busyness what do you say drives your behavior and motivates you to keep up a pattern of busyness? If, however, you are mostly productive what safeguards have you put in place to maintain this balanced lifestyle?

_____

_____

_____

_____

_____

_____

2. When you are busy for the sake of being busy, how is pride driving your behavior?

_____

_____

_____

3. Are you getting enough rest? If not, what will you do to make this a regular part of your daily renewal?

_____

_____

_____

4. What activities or circumstances is the Holy Spirit urging you to eliminate? Are there certain relationships you need to sever? Will you obey His leading? Why or why not?

_____

_____

_____

Prayer request(s):

_____

_____

_____

How my prayer(s) was answered:

_____

_____

_____

Peculiar Am I

But ye are a chosen generation, a royal priesthood,
an holy nation, a peculiar people;
that ye should shew forth the praises of him who hath
called you out of darkness
into his marvellous light;
(I Peter 2:9, KJV)

POINT TO PONDER: God is preparing me for my next phase in Him, but I must first accept the "me" that He has called me to be.

SCRIPTURES TO REFERENCE: I Peter 2:4-10

QUESTIONS TO ANSWER:

1. Can you relate to Dr. Celeste's sentiment about being different? If so, in what ways are you different? Are you okay with that?

   _____

   _____

   _____

   _____

2. What personality or character traits do you find most challenging to accept?

_____

_____

_____

3. In what way might being different positively influence your ability to fulfill the call that God has on your life?

_____

_____

_____

4. We have the power to speak life. Identify at least one person you can encourage that is struggling with being different? What will you say to encourage him/her? What portion of your testimony could you share that would help them embrace their uniqueness?

_____

_____

_____

_____

Prayer request(s):

_____

_____

_____

How my prayer(s) was answered:

_____

_____

_____

God's Friend

I love those who love me,
And those who seek me diligently will find me.
(Proverbs 8:17)

POINT TO PONDER: A meaningful relationship with God includes seeking His advice first.

SCRIPTURES TO REFERENCE: Proverbs 8:17; Isaiah 58:9a

QUESTIONS TO ANSWER:

1. What is your first reaction when you have a dilemma? Do you first discuss it with family and friends then go to God or do you go to God first?

   _____

   _____

   _____

   _____

2. God speaks to us differently, but He can often be heard as a still small voice speaking to our spirits. Have you learned to hear God's voice for yourself?

   _____

   _____

_____

_____

_____

3. How do you know when He is speaking to you? Besides a still small voice what other ways could He speak to you?

_____

_____

_____

_____

4. Do you consider yourself God's friend? What steps will you take to draw even closer to Him?

_____

_____

_____

_____

Prayer request(s):

_____

_____

_____

How my prayer(s) was answered:

_____

_____

_____

DAY 13

Personal Time with God

Scripture(s):

_____

_____

_____

_____

_____

How is the spirit speaking to you?

_____

_____

_____

_____

_____

DAY 14

Personal Time with God

Scripture(s):

_____

_____

_____

_____

_____

How is the spirit speaking to you?

_____

_____

_____

_____

_____

I Declare War!

For we do not wrestle against flesh and blood,
but against principalities,
against powers, against the rulers of the darkness of this age,
against spiritual hosts of wickedness in the heavenly places.
(Ephesians 6:12, KJV)

POINT TO PONDER: I won't take Satan's tactics lying down; I'll get on my knees and exercise the authority that Christ has given me.

SCRIPTURES TO REFERENCE: Ephesians 6:10-12; James 4:7; I John 4:4

QUESTIONS TO ANSWER:

1. Spiritual warfare is real. The enemy is determined to discourage you from completing this fast. In what ways has He challenged your faith? What safeguards have you or will you put in place to secure your successful completion of this fast?

_____

_____

_____

_____

2. It always helps to recall past victories. Have there been other times that you felt like you were in a war or spiritual battle? What was the outcome? What did you do to stay strengthened?

_____

_____

_____

3. What we believe is often evident in how we behave. Earlier Dr. Celeste mentioned how important it is to exhibit self-control, especially when it comes to controlling your emotions. How are you behaving during this fast? Are you grumbling and complaining or confident and positive?

_____

_____

_____

4. Do you wholeheartedly believe that God has given you power over the enemy? If yes, does your thoughts and behavior reflect a heart of belief?

_____

_____

_____

Prayer request(s):

_____

_____

How my prayer(s) was answered:

_____

_____

Superhuman

But those who wait on the LORD
Shall renew their strength;
They shall mount up with wings like eagles,
They shall run and not be weary,
They shall walk and not faint.
(Isaiah 40:31)

POINT TO PONDER: Today I declare that I can be super human if I simply wait on God and let His supernatural power work in my life.

SCRIPTURES TO REFERENCE: Isaiah 40:26-31, 55:11

QUESTIONS TO ANSWER:

1. How are you at waiting? Do you want everything right now or have you learned to wait on God? In what ways can you improve your attitude during your wait time?

_____

_____

_____

_____

2. What are you waiting for the Lord to do in your life? How long have you been waiting? What is most challenging about the wait? Do you trust God to do for you what He said He will do?

_____

_____

_____

_____

_____

3. Like Dr. Celeste, have you ever received news about a situation that was contrary to the word that God had given you? What did you do? Did you compromise or did you wait? What was the outcome?

_____

_____

_____

_____

_____

Prayer request(s):

_____

_____

_____

_____

How my prayer(s) was answered:

_____

_____

_____

_____

DAY 17

The God in Me

The ark of the LORD remained in the house of
Obed-Edom the Gittite three months.
And the LORD blessed Obed-Edom and all his household.
(II Samuel 6:11)

POINT TO PONDER: If I'm willing to endure a little discomfort for a season, others will have the awesome opportunity to see God in me and be blessed beyond measure.

SCRIPTURES TO REFERENCE: 2 Samuel 6:11; 2 Corinthians 3:17

QUESTIONS TO ANSWER:

1. Have you been or are you now in a place where you would rather not be? Explain your situation.

_____

_____

_____

_____

2. If you are in a challenging situation now, are you representing God well?

_____

_____

_____

_____

_____

3. Are others being blessed because you are in their presence? Are they able to see the love of God radiating from you? If not, what will you do to be a better representation of God?

_____

_____

_____

_____

_____

Prayer request(s):

_____

_____

_____

_____

How my prayer(s) was answered:

_____

_____

_____

_____

The Keys for Good Relationships

Behold, how good and how pleasant it is
for brethren to dwell together in unity!
(Psalm 133:1)

POINT TO PONDER: God designed me to be in healthy relationships and to dwell in unity.

SCRIPTURES TO REFERENCE: Psalm 133; Matthew 18:15a

QUESTIONS TO ANSWER:

1. How would you rate the quality of your relationships? Are they healthy and thriving or challenging and conflict-filled? What can you do to improve your relationships?

   _____

   _____

   _____

   _____

2. Is one or more of your relationships strained? What caused the strain and how did you play a part in all of this? What will you do to make it right?

   _____

_____

_____

_____

3. Ultimately the quality of our relationships is a reflection of the relationship we have with God. What is your relationship like with God? Are you making time to seek Him?

_____

_____

_____

_____

4. If you don't love yourself, loving someone else is nearly impossible. How do you feel about you? Are there some unresolved issues that you need to address? Where will you start? Speak with your accountability partner about what the spirit is revealing to you about yourself.

_____

_____

_____

_____

Prayer request(s):

_____

_____

_____

How my prayer(s) was answered:

_____

_____

_____

I Still Surrender

*And they overcame him by the blood of the Lamb
and by the word of their testimony.*
(Revelation 12:11a)

POINT TO PONDER: I will be the victor if I faint not. I'm almost to the finish line; I'll see it through to the end.

SCRIPTURE TO REFERENCE: Revelation 12:11a

QUESTIONS TO ANSWER:

1. Have you been tempted to give up on this fast? How do you think your continued surrender will benefit you in the long run?

_____

_____

_____

_____

2. We all have had struggles. What childhood challenges influence the way you operate as an adult.

_____

_____

_____

_____

_____

3. Sometimes it's embarrassing to share with another person what
   we are struggling with, but the scripture tells us that we overcome
   by the words of our testimony. Share with your accountability
   partner or other close friend one of your current challenges. How
   difficult will that be? How do you think it will help you?

_____

_____

_____

_____

_____

Prayer request(s):

_____

_____

_____

_____

How my prayer(s) was answered:

_____

_____

_____

_____

DAY 20

Personal Time with God

Scripture(s):

_____

_____

_____

_____

_____

How is the spirit speaking to you?

_____

_____

_____

_____

_____

Personal Time with God

Scripture(s):

_____

_____

_____

_____

_____

How is the spirit speaking to you?

_____

_____

_____

_____

_____

Dust Off Your Dreams

For a dream comes through much activity,
and a fool's voice is known by his many words.
(Ecclesiastes 5:3)

POINT TO PONDER: Trust that God has it all handled and He will provide the means. All He needs from me is my willingness to comply with His every command.

SCRIPTURES TO REFERENCE: Ecclesiastes 5:3; Habakkuk 2:2-4

QUESTIONS TO ANSWER:

1. What are your dreams? Write them down here or on another piece of paper. Are you on the road to fulfilling them? If not, what is holding you back?

    _____

    _____

    _____

    _____

    _____

2. Review your list above. Choose one dream and write out specific steps that you need to take to make this dream a reality.

For example:

I want to be a Surgical Tech

Step 1: Research the qualifications needed to be a surgical tech.

Step 2: Talk with a surgical tech to get their opinion about the field.

Step 3: Apply to schools.

Do this for each one of your dreams. Write you the steps that you need to follow below.

_____

_____

_____

3. For many different reasons, people fear telling others about their dreams. Don't let that be you. Pick one of the dreams you listed in Question 2. Tell your accountability partner or a close friend about that dream. How did it feel to tell someone else? How did they respond?

_____

_____

_____

Prayer request(s):

_____

_____

_____

How my prayer(s) was answered:

_____

_____

DAY 23

Your Breakthrough Is Coming Through

Then it happened, as he drew back his hand,
that his brother came out unexpectedly;
and she said, "How did you break through?
This breach be upon you!"
Therefore his name was called Perez.
(Genesis 38:29)

POINT TO PONDER: I am the victor and not the conquered, the head and not the tail, above and not beneath.

SCRIPTURES TO REFERENCE: Genesis 38; Deuteronomy 28; Matthew 1:3a

QUESTIONS TO ANSWER:

1. Are you in need of a breakthrough? Do you believe that God can and will deliver your from whatever you are challenged by right now? What will you do to keep your faith strong?

_____

_____

_____

_____

2. Who has been your "Judah"? What did they do? In what way, if any, does this hurt still affect you today?

_____

_____

_____

_____

_____

3. God doesn't waste pain. Tamar was rewarded handsomely for the hurt that she endured at the hand of Judah. Can you see how the hurts of your life have been or will be for God's greater plan? In not, pray and ask God to open the eyes of your heart so that you can see some of what He has in store for you.

_____

_____

_____

_____

_____

Prayer request(s):

_____

_____

_____

_____

How my prayer(s) was answered:

_____

_____

_____

DAY 24

The Answered Prayer

Then Eli answered and said,
"Go in peace, and the God of Israel grant your petition
which you have asked of Him."
(I Samuel 1:17)

POINT TO PONDER: I'll be content with today, praise God for what He has already done, and wait expectantly, without worry, for what is to come.

SCRIPTURES TO REFERENCE: I Samuel 1:8-18; I Peter 3:12

QUESTIONS TO ANSWER:

1. What specific requests have you put before God during the course of this fast? Do you believe that He will answer your prayers?

---

2. How is your thought life? During times of stress do you allow the enemy to bombard you with negative thoughts? Do you find solace in complaining? If you answered yes to either of those questions, what might you do differently the next time you are stressed about a particular situation?

_____

_____

_____

_____

_____

Prayer request(s):

_____

_____

_____

_____

How my prayer(s) was answered:

_____

_____

_____

_____

The Dead Will Live

As soon as Jesus heard the word that was spoken,
He said to the ruler of the synagogue,
"Do not be afraid; only believe."
(Mark 5:36)

POINT TO PONDER: It ain't over, until God says it's over. He has the final say.

SCRIPTURES TO REFERENCE: Proverbs 24:10; Joel 2:25-26; Mark 5:21-43; Romans 4:17

QUESTIONS TO ANSWER:

1. We are all in need of prayer. Name the specific ways your accountability partner can pray for you this week then ask him/her to pray with you.

   _____

   _____

   _____

   _____

2. Can you recall a time when you thought all hope was lost yet God resurrected a dead situation in your life? What was that situation and how did God turn it around for you?

_____

_____

_____

_____

3. The Word says that if you faint in the day of adversity your strength is small (see Proverbs 24:10) . How do you handle adversity? Do you give up easily or forge ahead knowing that God has the final say?

_____

_____

_____

_____

4. Do you currently have a dead situation in your life? What is it? Do you believe that God can resurrect it?

_____

_____

_____

_____

Prayer request(s):

_____

_____

_____

How my prayer(s) was answered:

_____

_____

_____

What Is for Me Is for Me

He shall be like a tree
Planted by the rivers of water,
that brings forth its fruit in its season,
whose leaf also shall not wither;
and whatever he does shall prosper.
(Psalm 1:3)

POINT TO PONDER: When I walk according to God's plan, I can't miss out.

SCRIPTURES TO REFERENCE: Deuteronomy 28:1-2; Psalm 1:3, 37:4, 23; Isaiah 55:11; 2 Corinthians 10:1-6

QUESTIONS TO ANSWER:

1. The mind is the battleground of the enemy. How often do you allow the enemy to have free reign of your thoughts? What will you do to gain better control over what you are thinking?

_____

_____

_____

_____

_____

2. How confident are you that what God has for you is for you?
   Are there times when you compare yourself to others and become
   discouraged? How has God proven to you that His plan for you
   will come to pass?

   _____

   _____

   _____

   _____

   _____

3. List some of the promises that God has made to you. Thank
   Him for these promises and ask Him to give you peace as you
   patiently wait for the manifestation of His promises.

   _____

   _____

   _____

   _____

   _____

Prayer request(s):

   _____

   _____

   _____

   _____

How my prayer(s) was answered?

   _____

   _____

   _____

   _____

Personal Time with God

Scripture(s):

_____
_____
_____
_____
_____

How is the spirit speaking to you?

_____
_____
_____
_____
_____

Personal Time with God

Scripture(s):

_____
_____
_____
_____
_____

How is the spirit speaking to you?

_____
_____
_____
_____
_____

DAY 29

The God of the Impossible

But Jesus looked at them and said to them,
"With men this is impossible, but with God all things are possible."
(Matthew 19:26)

POINT TO PONDER: In this season, God is calling me to a level of radical faith that far exceeds my previous dealings with Him.

SCRIPTURES TO REFERENCE: Matthew 19:23-30; Luke 17:6; John 14:13-14

QUESTIONS TO ANSWER:

1. What is faith? How has God tested your faith recently? What was the situation? Did the test draw you closer to God or cause you to move away. What do you need to do to increase you faith in God?

   _____

   _____

   _____

   _____

   _____

   _____

   _____

2. What bold and courageous declarations will you make today? What impossible thing do you believe God will do for you?

_____

_____

_____

_____

_____

3. Sometimes in our zeal we overstate God's will. How will you feel at the end of the fast if things don't turn about the way you envisioned? Will you still trust God to do the impossible?

_____

_____

_____

_____

_____

Prayer request(s):

_____

_____

_____

_____

How my prayer(s) was answered:

_____

_____

_____

DAY 30

Little Time Needed

"For My thoughts are not your thoughts,
nor are your ways my ways," says the LORD.
(Isaiah 55:8)

POINT TO PONDER: God doesn't need a lot of time.

SCRIPTURES TO REFERENCE: Isaiah 55:8; Jeremiah 17:5-8

QUESTIONS TO ANSWER:

1. Yesterday's blog post asked you to write down what you believe God will do for you before this fast's end. Did you do that? If not, what stopped you from making a declaration?

_____

_____

_____

_____

_____

_____

2. The old saying goes, "He may not come when you want, but He is always on time." Do you believe this to be true? Can you recall a time when you thought all hope was gone? Did things

eventually work out for you? What lessons did you learn from that particular circumstance?

_____

_____

_____

_____

_____

_____

_____

Prayer request(s):

_____

_____

_____

_____

How my prayer(s) was answered:

_____

_____

_____

_____

DAY 31

Grace and Glory

For by grace you have been saved through faith,
and that not of yourselves;
it is the gift of God, not of works, lest anyone should boast.
(Ephesians 2:8-9)

POINT TO PONDER: Without God's grace we would still be dead in our sins, wallowing in a sea of defeat and desperation.

SCRIPTURES TO REFERENCE: Ephesians 2:1-10; James1:5

QUESTIONS TO ANSWER:

1. As the song implies, "All the glory belongs to God." What does that mean to you? Take a moment to write down one thing God has done for you in the last week; the last month; and the last year.

    _____

    _____

    _____

    _____

    _____

2. Are you one to allow God's grace to operate in your life or do you try to do most things in your own strength?

    _____

_____

_____

_____

_____

3. Have you or are you now in God's way? Identify how.

_____

_____

_____

4. For which challenging situations do you need to leave more room for God's grace to operate? What will you do so that God has complete control?

_____

_____

_____

_____

Prayer request(s):

_____

_____

_____

How my prayer(s) was answered:

_____

_____

_____

Act Like You Are About to Move

*"Pass through the camp and command the people, saying,
'Prepare provisions for yourselves, for within three days
you will cross over this Jordan, to go in to possess
the land which the LORD your God is giving you to possess.'"*
(Joshua 1:11)

POINT TO PONDER: Step out in faith; prepare my provisions, and ACT LIKE I'm ABOUT TO MOVE.

SCRIPTURE TO REFERENCE: Joshua 1:11

QUESTIONS TO ANSWER:

1. What does the phrase ACT LIKE YOU ARE ABOUT TO MOVE mean to you?

    _____

    _____

    _____

    _____

2. It is said that preparation plus opportunity equals success. Think of one dream that God has placed in your heart. In what ways are you preparing for the manifestation of that dream?

    _____

_____
_____
_____
_____
_____

3. What signs have God shown you to let you know that He is
   ready to work on your behalf?

_____
_____
_____
_____
_____

Prayer request(s):

_____
_____
_____
_____

How my prayer(s) was answered:

_____
_____
_____
_____

The Promise

*And everyone who has left houses
or brothers or sisters or father or mother or wife or children or lands,
for my name's sake, shall receive a hundredfold,
and inherit eternal life.
(Matthew 19:29)*

POINT TO PONDER: If I would allow Gods' grace to empower my every action, God will get the glory, and I will receive all that God has promised, even a hundredfold." Amen.

SCRIPTURES TO REFERENCE: Exodus 20:2; Matthew 19:23-30; Ephesians 3:20

QUESTIONS TO ANSWER:

1. What sacrifices have you made in the past? In what way(s) did God reward you for your sacrifice(s)?

_____

_____

_____

_____

_____

_____

2. Are there people or situations that you put before God? If yes, who are they and what will you do to make this right?

_____

_____

_____

_____

_____

3. How do you feel about there being one last week? Has this process helped you to feel closer to God? Have you noticed changes in yourself and others? List those changes here.

_____

_____

_____

_____

_____

Prayer request(s):

_____

_____

_____

_____

How my prayer(s) was answered:

_____

_____

_____

_____

_____

DAY 34

Personal Time with God

Scripture(s):

_____

_____

_____

_____

_____

How is the spirit speaking to you?

_____

_____

_____

_____

_____

DAY 35

Personal Time with God

Scripture(s):

_____

_____

_____

_____

_____

How is the spirit speaking to you?

_____

_____

_____

_____

_____

DAY 36

No More Props

*FOR BEHOLD, the Lord, the Lord of hosts,
is taking away from Jerusalem and from Judah the stay
and the staff [every kind of prop],
the whole stay of bread and the whole stay of water,
(Isaiah 3:1, Amplified Bible)*

POINT TO PONDER: Depending solely on other people to hear a word from God is childish. It is time that I hear, believe, and speak God's truth as He has spoken it to me.

SCRIPTURES TO REFERENCE: Isaiah 3:1; I Corinthians 13:11

QUESTIONS TO ANSWER:

1. What are the props that are in your life?

_____

_____

_____

_____

_____

_____

2. A benefit of releasing your props is the ability to hear God for yourself and to have a closer, more intimate relationship with

Him. Is God telling you that it is time to let Him remove the props? Are you willing to let go? Why or why not?

_____

_____

_____

_____

_____

3. What do you anticipate your life will be like without the props?

_____

_____

_____

_____

_____

Prayer request(s):

_____

_____

_____

_____

How my prayer(s) was answered:

_____

_____

_____

_____

DAY 37

Reject Rejection

"Whoever listens to you listens to me;
whoever rejects you rejects me;
but whoever rejects me rejects him who sent me."
(Luke 10:16)

POINT TO PONDER: He will use me to call into existence that which is not, to move mountains in faith, and to draw men to Him.

SCRIPTURES TO REFERENCE: Luke 10:1-20

QUESTIONS TO ANSWER:

1. How do you handle rejection? Are you easily wounded by another's rejection or can you shake it off and move on? If the former, how will the scriptures in Luke 10 help you to better deal with rejection?

_____

_____

_____

_____

_____

_____

2. Do you sense God calling you to do something radical like Dr. Celeste's dad? What is it? Will you be obedient to God's command?

_____

_____

_____

_____

3. Isn't being reminded that the demons are subject to Jesus encouraging? Will this truth allow you to release fear so that you are better able to follow God's commands no matter the potential for rejection?

_____

_____

_____

_____

4. In which area of your life will you work on releasing fear?

_____

_____

_____

Prayer request(s):

_____

_____

_____

How my prayer(s) was answered:

_____

_____

_____

Childlike Humility

Therefore, whoever takes the lowly position of this child
is the greatest in the kingdom of heaven.
(Matthew 18:4)

POINT TO PONDER: That is what my heavenly father requires of me: a complete surrender and trust of His plan.

SCRIPTURES TO REFERENCE: Matthew 18:1-5; Revelation 2:17

QUESTIONS TO ANSWER:

1. How is surrendering your will a demonstration of humility?

   _____

   _____

   _____

   _____

   _____

2. Why do you think humility is so important to God? In which areas of your life could you exercise more humility?

   _____

   _____

   _____

_____

_____

3. Humility is necessary for us to be in healthy relationships. Romans 12:3 reads, "For I say, through the grace given to me, to everyone who is among you, not to think *of himself* more highly than he ought to think, but to think soberly, as God has dealt to each one a measure of faith." How do you think having humility in your relationships will strengthen them?

_____

_____

_____

_____

_____

Prayer request(s):

_____

_____

_____

_____

How my prayer(s) was answered:

_____

_____

_____

_____

DAY 39

Wait on the Lord

"So I will restore to you the years that the swarming locust has eaten,
the crawling locust,
the consuming locust,
and the chewing locust,
my great army which I sent among you.
And praise you shall eat in plenty and be satisfied,
the name of the LORD your God,
Who has dealt wondrously with you;
and my people shall never be put to shame."
(Joel 2:25-26)

POINT TO PONDER: Wait on the Lord and be of good courage.

SCRIPTURES TO REFERENCE: I Kings 8:56; Joshua 21:45; Joel 2:18-27

QUESTIONS TO ANSWER:

1. God will restore all that the locust has eaten. What area(s) of your life are in need of repair and restoration?

_____

_____

_____

_____

_____

2. During the course of this fast, how has God made changes in your circumstances?

_____

_____

_____

_____

_____

3. How do you see God continuing to restore over the course this year? In five years? In ten years?

_____

_____

_____

_____

_____

Prayer request(s):

_____

_____

_____

_____

How my prayer(s) was answered:

_____

_____

_____

God Has Done a New Thing

"Oh, give thanks to the LORD!"
(Psalm 105:1a)

Welcome to Day 40!

In the days to come, it's important that you take the time to appreciate what God has done and make note of all the changes that have occurred in you and around you while you were fasting.

Over the next couples of days, write down your key takeaways from the Fast. For example:

- ▶ What changed for you?
- ▶ In what way do you feel closer to God and more in line with His plan for you?
- ▶ Did your relationship(s) improve, how and with whom?
- ▶ What transitions happened during this time?
- ▶ What dreams, if any, have been rekindled?

I pray that you have allowed Him to do a new thing in you.

Until we meet again, stay surrendered for life!

About the Author

*D*r. **Celeste Owens**. Once, a little girl in the 7th grade read something about someone else's pain. Her purpose was clear, to help those that have been hurt and mangled by life. It was in that moment that Celeste knew she would become a psychologist. Her sensitivity to the distress of others framed her life purpose to assist in improving the quality of life for all those who God allowed to her to intercept paths with.

Dr. Celeste practiced as a psychologist for more than 10 years, but when God instructed her to leave it all behind, she did. Today she is reaping the benefits of her obedience. Although her career focus has changed — she is now a motivational speaker, health advocate, and author — her passion to help others live his/her best life has not.

In 2012, she and her husband Andel co-founded Dr. Celeste Owens Ministries, LLC who's calling hearts back to God through surrender of spirit, mind and body. They believe that surrender is a lifestyle and a necessary posture for today's Christian.

An accomplished scholar, Dr. Celeste holds a Bachelor of Arts in Psychology from the State University of New York at Buffalo, a Master of Science in Applied Counseling Psychology from the

University of Baltimore and a Doctorate of Philosophy in Counseling Psychology from the University of Pittsburgh. In 2013, Dr. Celeste became a Certified Natural Health Professional.

Dr. Celeste resides in the surrounding Washington Metropolitan Area where her most important works are being wife to her husband of 17 years and mom to their two children.

Printed in the USA
CPSIA information can be obtained
at www.ICGtesting.com
LVHW011639271223
767218LV00006B/191